Insults Aren't Funny

What to Do About Verbal Bullying

by Amanda F. Doering

pictures by Simone Shin

PICTURE WINDOW BOOKS
a capstone imprint

Note to Parents and Educators

Bullying has serious, long-term consequences for both the person who is bullied and the person who bullies. For bullying to stop, kids and adults must learn to recognize bullying behavior, and develop immediate and fair ways of dealing with it.

Kids often tease each other or call each other nicknames. When done in a friendly manner, this behavior can be fun. However, name-calling, insults, and threats are examples of verbal bullying and should not be tolerated.

While reading this book, encourage the child to talk about his or her own experiences with verbal bullying. Has the child experienced verbal bullying, witnessed someone being bullied, or acted as a bully? What did the child do in these situations? Did he or she handle the situations correctly?

Thanks to our adviser for her expertise, research, and advice:
Dorothy L. Espelage, PhD
Department of Educational Psychology
University of Illinois, Urbana-Champaign

Editor: Michelle Hasselius
Designer: Lori Bye
Creative Director: Nathan Gassman
Production Specialist: Laura Manthe
The illustrations in this book were created digitally.

Picture Window Books are published by Capstone,
1710 Roe Crest Drive, North Mankato, Minnesota 56003
www.capstonepub.com

Copyright © 2016 by Picture Window Books, a Capstone imprint. All rights reserved. No part of this publication may be reproduced in whole or in part, or stored in a retrieval system, or transmitted in any form or by any means, electronic, mechanical, photocopying, recording, or otherwise, without written permission of the publisher.

Design elements: Shutterstock:JungleOutThere

Library of Congress Cataloging-in-Publication Data
Doering, Amanda F., 1980–
Insults aren't funny : what to do about verbal bullying / by Amanda F. Doering.
pages cm. — (Picture Window Books. No more bullies)
Summary: "Sensitive, narrative text from illustrated animal characters shows readers what verbal bullying is and provides possible solutions to stop it"—Provided by publisher.
ISBN 978-1-4795-6942-7 (library binding)
ISBN 978-1-4795-6958-8 (paperback)
ISBN 978-1-4795-6962-5 (eBook PDF)
1. Bullying—Juvenile literature. 2. Invective—Juvenile literature. 3. Aggressiveness in children—Juvenile literature. I. Title.
BF637.B85T68 2016
302.34'3—dc23   2014048700

Soccer is my favorite sport. I've been playing on an after-school team since I was little. I really like playing goalie. I'm not the best player, but I have a lot of fun. At least I used to.

This year we're playing with older kids. Most of them are nice. But one player, Dana, can be mean. During games, Dana gets angry and calls me names if I make a mistake. Soccer used to be fun, but now it just makes me nervous.

We have a game this morning. During warm-ups, I hear a voice near me.
"Hey, Casey! I mean, dorkface!"

It's Dana. I pretend I don't hear and run to the field.

"Hey I'm talking to you, fatso," Dana says. "You'd better not screw up today. I want to win!"

"But ... but it's not all up to me," I say.

"But it's not all up to me," Dana repeats in a high, whiny voice. "You'd better not mess up—or else!" Dana threatens, zooming ahead of me.

A good way to avoid bullying is to use the buddy system. Stick by a friend in places bullying occurs. Do the same for a friend who is being bullied.

Dana's words make it hard to concentrate. I can't even pay attention to what Coach Barnes is saying. He tells us our positions. I have to ask him to repeat mine.

"Remember what I said, stupid," Dana whispers to me on the field. "No mistakes!"

I nod, trying to hold back tears. I have to play well today, even if my stomach is in knots.

During the game, my friend Reese passes the ball to me. My heart pounds. It's time to show Dana what I can do. But before I get a chance, a player from the other team steals the ball.

"Casey, you're so slow!" Dana growls, running after the ball.

The other team scores a goal. "**You're as bad as Casey!**" I hear Dana yell at the goalie.

Dana's words ring in my ears. Maybe I *am* really bad. Maybe I shouldn't play soccer anymore.

Repeated name-calling and insults are very hurtful. People who are bullied can start to believe what they hear, even if it isn't true.

It's my turn to play goalie. The score is tied 1 to 1, with five minutes left in the game. I'm so nervous, I feel like throwing up.

Dana and Reese keep the ball on the other team's side. But they can't score. Now there are only two minutes left.

Uh-oh. The other team has the ball. They're heading my way. The players weave in and out. I lose track of the ball until it sails past my head into the net behind me. Time runs out. The other team wins the game.

It's bad enough that we lost the game. But I know Dana will blame me.

"Nice job, dummy!" Dana shouts sarcastically after the others are gone. "Casey, you stink! You're not a rabbit. You're a turtle!"

I feel terrible. I start to cry. It makes things worse.

"Crying won't help, baby," Dana says. "Wah, wah!" Dana mocks me and walks away.

Everyone thinks I'm crying because of the game. But we've lost games before. It's just that no one has made me feel bad about losing before.

It can be hard not to cry or show fear when being bullied. But the person who is bullying wants you to feel upset and afraid. If you can pretend you're not upset or ignore the bully, he or she might give up.

Coach Barnes tells us we played a really tough team. The rest of my teammates aren't mean to me, but I can tell they're disappointed.

"It's not your fault, Casey. We all lost the game," says Reese.

"Dana blames me," I sniff.

"Dana's being a bully," Reese says. "I think you should talk to Coach Barnes about it."

I shake my head no. "That will just make things worse," I say. "I think I should just quit soccer."

"But you love soccer!" Reese says. "We have so much fun playing."

"Not anymore," I say.

If you or someone else is being bullied, it's always best to tell an adult you trust. The adult can stop the bullying behavior and get everyone the help he or she needs.

On Monday I'm afraid to face Dana at soccer practice. I call my dad and tell him I'm sick. He picks me up so I don't have to go.

On Wednesday Coach Barnes finds me in the hallway after school.

"Casey, Reese told me that you're thinking about quitting soccer," Coach Barnes says. I nod. "Reese also said it's because Dana is being mean to you," he says.

Coach Barnes puts his arm around me. "I'm very sorry you've been bullied, Casey," he says. "Sports should be fun, and teammates should support each other. I promise to put an end to this, OK?"

Before practice, Coach Barnes sits the team down. He explains that calling people names, saying mean things, and threatening people are examples of bullying. Coach Barnes tells us how to be good teammates. He also says that anyone caught bullying another player will sit out a game.

Reese winks at me. I smile back.
I hope this works.

Coach Barnes thinks I should tell my parents about being bullied. He says he will help me.

"Verbal bullying can be just as hurtful as physical bullying," says Coach Barnes during the meeting with my parents.

I nod. I know how bad it feels. Coach Barnes says that I might feel sad for a while. If I do, I should talk to him, my parents, or the counselor at school.

"And tell one of us if this happens again. OK, Casey?" Coach Barnes says.

People who have been bullied often feel sad or bad about themselves. This can last a long time. Some people need help to get over these feelings. If you've been bullied, talk to a parent or school counselor about how you feel.

Dana had to sit out of today's game because of bullying. I was worried that everyone would think I tattled. But no one said anything, including Dana.

"You were right about telling Coach Barnes, Reese," I say after the game. "Thanks for doing that."

"That's what friends are for," says Reese. "Good game!"

It's nice to have so many people on my side. I'm feeling better already. I think playing soccer will be fun again soon.

Glossary

bully—to frighten or pick on someone over and over

concentrate—to focus your thoughts and attention on something

counselor—a person trained to help people with problems or give advice

insult—a hurtful remark

mock—to laugh at or make fun of by copying someone's actions or way of speaking

nervous—being worried and afraid about what might happen

sarcastic—using mocking words that are meant to hurt or make fun of someone or something

threaten—to say you will harm someone or something in the future

verbal—spoken or made up of words

Read More

Bracken, Beth. *The Little Bully.* Little Boost. North Mankato, Minn.: Picture Window Books, 2012.

Cook, Julia. *Tease Monster: A Book About Teasing vs. Bullying.* Building Relationships. Boys Town, Neb.: Boys Town Press, 2013.

McAneney, Caitie. *Bullies.* Let's Talk About It. New York: PowerKids Press, 2015.

Internet Sites

FactHound offers a safe, fun way to find Internet sites related to this book. All of the sites on FactHound have been researched by our staff.

Here's all you do:

Visit *www.facthound.com*

Type in this code: 9781479569427

Check out projects, games and lots more at www.capstonekids.com

Index

buddy system, 5
counselors, 20
crying, 6, 12, 13, 17
feelings, 3, 8, 10, 12, 13, 20, 22
friends, 5, 8, 14, 15, 19, 22
physical bullying, 20
talking to adults, 15, 16, 17, 18, 20, 22
tattling, 22

verbal bullying
   long-term effects of, 20
   types of, 3, 4, 5, 6, 8, 12, 19
   ways to stop, 5, 13, 15, 19

All of the books in the series:

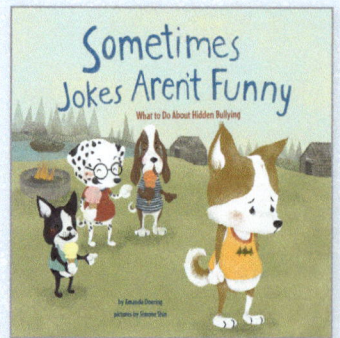
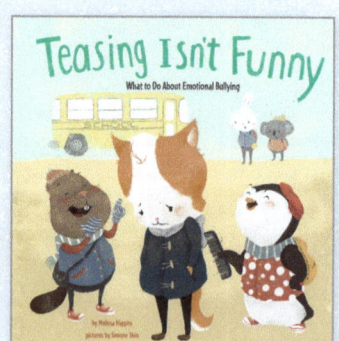